#8 Bride and Groom

AH!
WSH
TO-TOMARI-CHAN!

SMILE
にぱ。

SO...
I GUESS...
THE FEELING IS *MUTUAL* THEN, HUH?
HEH HEH...
SORRY...
....
UH...
ER...
I... DIDN'T MEAN TO *INTERRUPT* YOU.
....
HUH.
WOW... THAT'S... GREAT.

JUST... GREAT.
UM...
TO--
LATER!
TOMARI-CHAN!!

THANK YOU...
FOR ACCEPTING ME.

N YOU GROW UP?

I'M GOING TO BE TOMARI-CHAN'S *BRIDE*!
ぶ
HAZUMU, YOU ***DUMMY***! *BOYS* CAN'T BE BRIDES!

Sniff
BUT I WANNA ...!
WHOA! DON'T CRY!
BOYS GET TO BE "GROOMS" INSTEAD.
ummm...
THAT'S IT.
"GROOMS" ...?

THEN WHEN GROW UP...
I'LL BE YOUR GROOM!

WHY'D I HAVE TO REMEMBER THAT *NOW*...?
I MEAN, YOU CAN'T CALL THAT A PROMISE.
THEY WERE JUST... *WORDS* WE SAID WHEN WE WERE LITTLE.

SOMEWHERE DEEP DOWN INSIDE...
WAS I HOPING THERE WAS SOME TRUTH TO THEM?
UGH...

GRAAAAAH!!!!
POW!!
WOOOOOO
OH.
HEY, TOMARI--
WOP
BOUNCE
SOON, NAMIKO. **SOON!** IT WON'T BE LONG UNTIL YOU CAN LEAVE BEHIND THOSE 35 BOY-FRIENDLESS YEARS OF YOUR LIFE!
AHA!
FWOOSH

SORA-SENSEI!
PLEASE, ALLOW ME, TSUKI NAMIKO...
TO--
tmp tmp
KRIK
SPLOOSH
twitch
twitch
NGAA...
tmp tmp tmp
STOMP
STOMP
STOMP
IT APPEARS THAT "LOVE"...
IS A DIFFICULT EMOTION TO CONTROL.
PUU?

AFTER THAT DAY...

YASUNA-CHAN STARTED WALKING HOME WITH ME ALL THE TIME.

DAYS LATER--

WHY DON'T YOU GO EAT LUNCH WITH YASUNA?
WE CAN ALL EAT TOGETHER!
'kay?
AHA HA HA HA HA HA HA HA HA!
NAH, THAT'S OKAY. I'LL PASS.
I DON'T WANT TO... DISTURB YOU TWO, YOU KNOW.
WE'LL JUST GO EAT SOMEWHERE ELSE.
BESIDES, MAKING ME WATCH YOU TWO...
IS KINDA HARSH, DON'T YOU THINK?
SWAP
TOMA--
....

SORRY, GUYS.
I WAS A *REAL* BITCH BACK THERE, WASN'T I?
WELL...
YOU DO HAVE THAT RIGHT, AFTER ALL.
FOR NOW.
HOWEVER... I DON'T THINK YOU'LL BE ABLE...
TO KEEP *RUNNING* LIKE THAT FOREVER.

FSHHHHH
HEH HEH HEH...
HERE WE GO! IT'S TIME...
FOR SOME PERSONAL PARENTAL LOVE!!
GAK?!
FSHHHHH

IT CAN'T BE COINCIDENCE ANYMORE... TOMARI-CHAN'S AVOIDING ME!
sniff sniff
SHE'S MAD AT ME!
BUT WHY?
Is it because she walked in on us in the classroom that one day?
Why would she get upset about that?
NO, WAIT.
MAYBE SHE'S--?

SHE DIDN'T REALLY LOOK "MAD" AT ME.

IT WAS MORE LIKE SHE WAS ON THE VERGE OF ***TEARS***.

SHOOP

STOMP
CRACKLE~
HAZUMU? *AAAARGH!!* I DON'T HAVE MY GLASSES ON!! WHERE ARE MY GLASSES?!!
ACK!! MOM! DID YOU JUST STEP ON WHAT I *THINK* YOU DID?!

I'LL BE YOUR GROOM!
HA!
LIKE I'M GONNA LET SOME PANSY BE MY GROOM!
YOU'RE GONNA HAVE TO BE STRONG AND AWESOME AND MANLY FIRST!
THAT'S THE ONLY WAY YOU'RE GONNA GET TO BE MY GROOM.
AWW...
SO START ACTING MORE LIKE A BOY ALREADY!!
AND QUIT MAKIN' DAISY-CHAINS!

THAT'S RIGHT.

SHE'S ABSOLUTELY RIGHT.

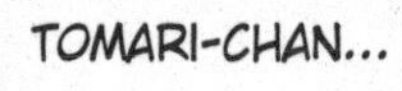
TOMARI-CHAN...

TNK
TNK

!

WHAT'S SHE DOING HERE ...?
TNK

I DON'T THINK YOU'LL BE ABLE TO KEEP RUNNING FOREVER.
GRRR...
HFF
WHAT-- HEY!
WHAT'RE YOU SOPPING WET FOR?
TOMARI-CHAN...
TOMARI-CHAN!
blink
YES?

I...
UM...
I... UH...

WHAT?! SPIT IT OUT ALREADY!
AH HA HA HA...
HOLD ON... GIVE ME A SEC, OKAY?

UM...
I KNOW YOU HAVE TO BE *PRETTY* MAD AT ME...

MAD? ABOUT *WHAT?*

SO YOU *ARE* MAD?
AND *HURT...?*

HUH...?
IT'S MY FAULT.
ISN'T IT?
WHAT ARE YOU--?
TOMARI-CHAN...
I CAME HERE TO APOLOGIZE.
IT WOULD BE NICE IF YOU LOOKED AT ME WHEN I TALK TO YOU!
YANK
What the--?
JERK!
ABOUT YASUNA-CHAN...
THERE ARE... REASONS...
WHY I DON'T WANT TO LEAVE HER ALONE.
I WANT TO BE WITH HER FOR HER OWN SAKE.

BUT...
I DON'T WANT THAT TO DRIVE US APART.

I DON'T WANT TO NOT BE ABLE TO TALK TO YOU.
I HATE IT!
I WANT US TO BE FRIENDS AGAIN, LIKE WE WERE BEFORE!
HUH ...?
YOU'RE IMPORTANT TO ME, TOMARI-CHAN.
YOU'RE MY FRIEND. I... L--
SMACK!

Oww...
Phoo
Phoo
QUIT SPOUTING CRAP LIKE THAT, OKAY?
I MEAN, YOU LOVE YASUNA, DON'T YOU?

THAT'S WHY YOU AND HER DID THAT. RIGHT?!

WELL... UH... TO TELL YOU THE TRUTH...
I DON'T KNOW.
HUH?!
YOU'RE BOTH **EQUALLY** IMPORTANT TO ME.
I'VE THOUGHT ABOUT IT, BUT I CAN'T DECIDE WHICH ONE OF YOU I LIKE MORE...
AND...
--OH! I'M SORRY, TOMARI-CHAN!
THIS **SO** ISN'T WORKING! I DON'T SOUND **MANLY** AT ALL!

NOW YOU'LL **NEVER** LET ME BE YOUR GROOM...!
WHAT DID YOU JUST SAY...?
HUH?
twitch
WHAT, DON'T YOU REMEMBER?
Eh heh... Now I'm embarrassed...

DAMMIT! THERE'S NO GETTING OUT OF THIS NOW!
YOU LIKE US **BOTH** THE SAME... RIGHT?
YEAH.
hup
SO... THAT MEANS...
YOU'D DO THE SAME THING FOR US BOTH, RIGHT?

SAME THING ...?
...
GYAAAAA?!
oh jeez!
ack!
THAT?! B-BUT I-I JUST KINDA SAT THERE, AND Y-YASUNA-CHAN CAME UP, AND-- ARGH!!
oh jeez!
GRAB

oh my god...
oh my god...
HUG...

TOMAR--
....
HUG
HEY, YOU KNOW WHAT? I'M A GIRL NOW, SO I REALLY CAN BECOME A BRIDE!
MORON...

ALL RIGHT... ALL RIGHT... I GIVE UP. I'LL ACCEPT IT.
I LOVE HAZUMU!
A LOT!!

JEEZ, IT'S NOT EVEN SUMMER VACATION YET, BUT IT'S ALREADY SCORCH-ING!
HEY! NOW THAT'S AN IDEA! WHY DON'T WE GO TO THE BEACH?
YEAH. I BET A DIP IN THE OCEAN WOULD FEEL REAL GOOD ABOUT NOW.
YEAH! WHY NOT? SUNDAY SOUNDS GOOD. LET'S GO FOR IT!
#9 A Trip to the Beach
IT STARTED OUT SO HARM-LESSLY...
JUST AN INNOCENT CONVER-SATION BETWEEN GUYS.

#9 A Trip to the Beach

BUT MY BEST FRIEND GOT TURNED INTO A GIRL A LITTLE WHILE AGO.

WHOA, WAIT!
HAZUMU IS MY BEST FRIEND!
I CAN'T LET DIRTY THOUGHTS BETRAY THE BOND OF FRIENDSHIP FORGED BETWEEN MEN!!
WHAT THE HELL AM I THINKING?!
DUMMY DUMMY
ASUTA?
WHAT'S WRONG?
UWAAA AAAA!!!
?
WHY ARE YOU SITTING OVER HERE ALL BY YOURSELF?
COME SIT WITH US AND TALK.
N-NO! THAT'S OKAY!
JUST LEMME ALONE!
why?
B-because...
tee hee
....

AH, WE'RE HERE...
THE BEACH!!
の家

hee hee

THE OCEAN...
URK
THE PRIMORDIAL SOUP FROM WHICH SPRUNG ALL LIFE ON THIS PLANET.

EVEN NOW, IT EVOKES FEELINGS OF "LOVE" LIKE FEW OTHER PLACES ON THIS WORLD.
CO--?!
SPLOOT
ACCORDING TO MY DATA, HUMANS BECOME SO OVERWHELMED BY "LOVE" WHEN NEAR THE OCEAN THAT THEY OFTEN COPULATE RIGHT UPON ITS SHORES.
WITH WHOM SHALL YOU CHOOSE TO PER-FORM?
I'm terribly intrigued...
NO-BODY!!

AND WHAT'S UP WITH *THAT* SWIM-SUIT...?
Where did you buy it?
ISN'T THAT JUST A CENTURY OR TWO OUT OF DATE, SENSEI?
IS IT?
MY DOCU-MENTATION HAD IT CATEGORIZED AS "THE HEIGHT OF FASHION." AH WELL...
And I did not purchase it. I *made* it.
I SHALL WEAR *THIS* INSTEAD.
ばりっ
SHRIP
GYAAAAARA
?
NOW THEN, EVERYONE, TO THE *OCEAN*!
yay!
ZOOOOM
SENSEI, NO!!!
drip drip
SORA-SENSEI, YOU'RE SO... SO... *BOLD!* ♡
I think I've died and gone to heaven...

HAZUMU!
HAZUMU-KUN...
LET'S GO!
SHALL WE GO?

....

GRIN

I JUST CAN'T CHOOSE BETWEEN THEM.

すーい
SWSH
すーい
SWSH
PUU PUU
HEY!

BA-
ASUTA!
THUMP
AHH!
SLIP
THAT WAS CLOSE...
AH--
AH--
steam steam
?
I'M GOING TO GET SOME DRINKS!!!
DASH
...?

GOTTA CALM DOWN! GOTTA CALM DOWN!!
SHE'S YOUR BEST FRIEND!
YOU CAN'T GO AROUND HAVING THOSE FEELINGS!
JEEZ, ASUTA'S SURE ACTING WEIRD TODAY.
--OH. HEY.
ARE YOU HAVING FUN?
HAZUMU-KUN.
YEAH.
KOFF KOFF KOFF
THIS... THIS IS MY FIRST TIME AT THE BEACH WITH SOME-ONE I LIKE.
ARE YOU ALL RIGHT?
Y-YEAH.
THINK I... SWALLOWED A LITTLE SEAWATER.
WHEW...

TIRED, TOMARI-CHAN?
WE WENT SWIMMING ALL THE TIME WHEN WE WERE LITTLE. REMEMBER?
Y-YEAH. IT'S BEEN A LONG TIME SINCE WE LAST WENT.
YEAH.
PLAYED REAL HARD THERE FOR A WHILE.
......
YOU KNOW WHAT?!
ZOOOOOM
I THINK I'LL GO HELP ASUTA WITH THOSE DRINKS!!
GOD... WHAT IS THIS?
IS IT "COUPLES' DAY" OR SOMETHING?
Feels kinda awkward...
......

BUT SOMEDAY, I'LL HAVE A GIRLFRIEND OF MY OWN AND--
POOOFF
ぽわわん
AAAARGH!!
NO! NO! NO!
ASUTA!!
BA-THUMP!
ドキ
YEAH?
HUH...?
WHAT? HIM?!
TURN
さっ
what the HELL
hmph.
Let's go try somewhere else.
Damn.
NYAAH!
SO YOU REALLY DO ALREADY HAVE A BOY-FRIEND?
BO--?!
YES!!
SORRY ABOUT USING YOU LIKE THAT, ASUTA.
THEY JUST WOULDN'T TAKE 'NO' FOR AN ANSWER.
HUH? YOU MEAN, THOSE GUYS...
WERE HITTING ON YOU?
YEAH. I COULD HARDLY BELIEVE IT!
THERE'S A LOT MORE TO BEING A GIRL THAN I THOUGHT...
They all go through so much!

MAKE THAT "LIKE ANY OTHER SUPER-HOT BABE"!!

DAMMIT...
SHE'S SO CUTE!
IF I WAS LIKE THOSE OTHER GUYS, AND DIDN'T KNOW HAZUMU FROM BEFORE...
NICE TO MEET YOU.
I WOULD'VE FALLEN FOR HER IN A HEART-BEAT.
I'M OSARAGI HAZUMU.
THAT'S IT, IF SHE'D ALWAYS BEEN A GIRL
BUT THAT'S NOT POSSIBLE FOR ME.
"ASUTA-KUN"?
IT'S A PLEASURE!
I DO KNOW HER. SHE'S BEEN MY BEST FRIEND FOR AGES.
SHE'S JUST A FRIEND. JUST A FRIEND!!
UM...
HELLO?
STMP STMP STMP STMP
DAMMIT! GO AWAY, PERVY THOUGHTS! GET LOST!
ASUTA?
ASUTA?
Shake
Shake
I'M SUCH A JERK! HOW CAN I DO THIS TO MY BEST FRIEND?!

ASUTA! WHERE ARE YOU GOING?!

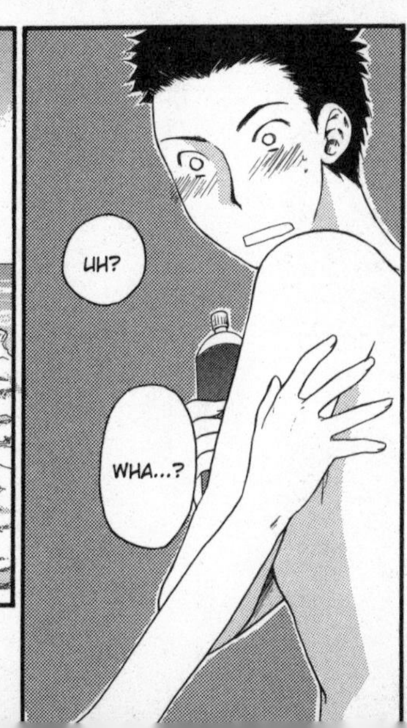
UH?
WHA...?

WHERE--?
WE'VE GONE WAY PAST WHERE THE OTHERS ARE.

WAY PAST EVERYBODY, ACTUALLY.

THERE'S **NOBODY** OUT THIS WAY AT ALL.
NOBODY ...?
HRM...
WILL ONE MAKE A MOVE?
PUU?
OH...
SENSEI! ♡
YES?
EEE! ♡

WHAT ARE YOU DOING UP HERE?
ALL OUR STUDENTS ARE BACK OVER *THERE*.
I HAVE A VERY *KEEN* INTEREST IN THE CONCEPT OF "LOVE," YOU SEE.
I WAS JUST *PONDERING* SOME OF ITS IMPLICATIONS.
L-LOVE...?
BA-THUMP
OF LATE, MY MIND HAS BEEN FILLED WITH NOTHING BUT THOUGHTS OF "LOVE."
IT IS SO, EVEN NOW...
EVEN AT THIS *VERY* MOMENT.
W-W-W-WHAAAAAAT?!!
DOES THAT MEAN THAT HE'S... HE'S... THINKING ABOUT *ME*?!

I, TSUKI NAMIKO, HAVE BEEN TRAPPED IN A BOYFRIEND-LESS *LIMBO* FOR ALL 35 YEARS OF MY LIFE.
BUT NOW, FINALLY... *FINALLY!* THE TIME HAS COME FOR ME TO PUT AN END TO THE WAITING!
Hazumu-Kun is taking an awfully long time...
......
UM...
YASUNA?
YES?
YOU KNOW, ABOUT...

ASUTA, WHAT'S GOTTEN INTO YOU?
YOU'VE...
BEEN ACTING WEIRD ALL DAY.

IT'S BE-CAUSE...
YOU'RE STUCK HANGING OUT WITH ME, ISN'T IT?
IT MUST BE EMBAR-RASSING, BEING AROUND ME NOW.
MAYBE EVEN A LITTLE... DISGUST-ING.

LIKE HELL IT'S EMBAR-RASSING!!
GRAB

HUH...?

HAZUMU.
I-I...

I THINK I'M...
PULL
FALLING--

AAAA AAAA AAAA AAH?!
SENSEI!
PU?
KA
SPLOOSH!
HAZUMU! WHAT'S WRONG?!
SENSEI!!
HAZUMU-KUN...!
NAMIKO-SENSEI JUST--!
ASUTA!!!
WHAT THE HELL'D YOU DO?!
POW
UGH...
IT SEEMS THAT TIMING IS A VERY IMPORTANT COMPONENT TO "LOVE."
?

boo-hoo..
PUU!
What is "love"!? Mumble mumble...
ZZZ
....

YASUNA...?
LISTEN...
I'M IN LOVE WITH HAZUMU TOO.
......
ZZZZ...
JUST SO YOU KNOW.

IT WAS SO FRAIL, SO *WEAK*...

#10 I'll Just Watch...

#10 I'll Just Watch...

SO IN OTHER WORDS, MY LOVELY STUDENTS...
WE'LL BE HAVING A *GREAT*, BIG, CLASS-WIDE DARE!
HUH?
THIS ABSOLUTELY FANTABULOUS IDEA IS COURTESY OF SORA-SENSEI, OF COURSE!
Eee!! clap clap clap clap ♡
UH... SENSEI ...?
YES, KURUSU-SAN!
AREN'T DARES LIKE THIS... SOMETHING YOU DO *ONLY* AROUND OBON?
SWISH
YES, BUT THIS IS *CLASS*!
RIGHT, SORA-SENSEI? ♡
CORRECT.
THIS "DARE" MAY BE BASED UPON THE ANCIENT JAPANESE CUSTOM OF "TESTS OF COURAGE," BUT IT IS *STILL* CLASS.
A VERY... *SPECIAL* CLASS.

I AM EXPECTING GREAT THINGS OF YOU... ALL OF YOU.
SIGH
He's looking right at me...
THUD

AW, MAN!!

I HATE DARES! I HATE 'EM, HATE 'EM, HATE 'EM!!
YEAH, I MEAN, YOU ALWAYS DID MAKE MOST SCAREDY-CATS LOOK BRAVE.
REALLY?

HECK YEAH! YOU SHOULD'VE SEEN IT WHEN WE'D GO TO HAUNTED HOUSES. HAZUMU'S UNBELIEVABLE!
Snicker
WHAT?!

HEY!
TOMARI-CHAN! KNOCK IT OFF!
HAZUMU? "UNBELIEV-ABLE"?!
AH HA HA HA HA HA HA
HAZUMU-KUN?

SHE'D GRAB ONTO ME AND STICK THERE LIKE GLUE! YOU COULDN'T HAVE GOTTEN HER OFF ME WITH A CROWBAR!
Oh, Asuta! I'm so scared!
Hush, now. No need to be afraid.
There, it's not so scary when we're together, now is it?
squeeze squeeze
NYAHA HA HA HA HA HA HA HA
SNORT
LET'S GO TOGETHER, HAZUMU-KUN. WOULDN'T THAT BE FUN?
Well... uh...
O-OKAY. WE'RE IN THE SAME GROUP AND ALL...
WOP
BY THE WAY, THIS IS WHAT REALLY HAPPENS...
Dammit, Hazumu!
Quit pulling already! You'll tear my dress!
Yammer Yammer
Me too!
Hee hee.
......
....

AW, MAN...
WHY ME...?
tp
tp
IT HASN'T EVEN STARTED YET, AND ALREADY I'M SCARED...
Sniff
PLUS, I JUST KNOW ALIEN-SAN HAS SOME WEIRD, ULTERIOR MOTIVE FOR THIS WHOLE THING TOO...
I'm so nervous I think I upset my stomach...
GLURGGLURG
HUH? AYUKI-CHAN...?
WHO'S THAT WITH HER?
MARI AYUKI-SAMA
I'M SORRY.

NARI AYUKI-SAMA
I DON'T USUALLY CONCERN MYSELF WITH THIS SORT-OF THING.
......
THERE'S SOMEONE ELSE YOU LIKE, ISN'T THERE?
YES...
OH JEEZ!
OH JEEZ!
BUT THAT'S NONE OF YOUR BUSINESS.
HUH?!
I GUESS NOT...

HAZUMU-KUN...?
ACK!
YES, MA'AM?!
FSH
I'M SORRY, AYUKI-CHAN...
I... UH...
DIDN'T MEAN TO EAVESDROP--
ON THE CONVERSATION ABOUT MY POTENTIAL RELATION-SHIPS?
I'M SO SORRY!!
BOW BOW
IT'S OKAY.
I, UH, THAT IS... D-DON'T GIVE UP, AYUKI-CHAN! GO FOR IT! KEEP TRYING!!
I STOPPED DOING THAT A *LONG* TIME AGO.
HUH...?
TRYING. I NEVER REALLY DID IT IN THE FIRST PLACE.

NOR DO I EVER INTEND TO START.

SENSEI
SLIP
WHUUMP
LET US TAKE THIS OPPORTUNITY TO MAKE SOME *DETAILED* OBSERVATIONS.
PUUUU! ♡

NNNNNGH
GOD, WOULD YOU WALK WITH YOUR EYES OPEN *ALREADY*? **SHEEZ.**
shudder shudder shudder
PEEEEK
blink blink blink

YAAAAAAAAAAH!
I CAN'T, I CAN'T, I CAN'T!! TOMARI-CHAN, I'M TOO SCARED!!!
WAAAAAH!
ALL RIGHT, ALL RIGHT! YOU CAN *HOLD* ONTO ME. THAT'LL MAKE YOU FEEL *BETTER*, RIGHT?!
My ARM, not my SHIRT! You'll rip it!

LET ME JUST STAY LIKE THIS!
When you move your right foot, I'll move my right foot. That'll work!
SQUEEZE
......
GOD...
NOT THAT I'M UPSET OR ANYTHING, BUT DO YOU HAVE ANY IDEA WHAT YOU JUST DID...?
HUH...?
....

UM...
DID I DO THAT WHEN I WAS A GUY TOO?
YES!
BUT YOU'RE A GIRL NOW, SO JUST FORGET ABOUT IT AND HOLD ON TO ME! GOT THAT?!

OH...!
YASUNA-CHAN...
HUH?!
ACK!
OH JEEZ...
squeeze
UMM...
NOW WHAT DO I DO?!

THIS IS *EXACTLY* WHAT ALIEN-SAN WANTED TO HAPPEN!
MMPH? A DARE?
tooth-brush
YES.
IT IS ABOUT TIME I COLLECTED SOME NEW DATA IN REGARDS TO YOUR ROMANTIC RELATIONSHIPS.
washa washa
FAFF AFFEN...?
(That again...?)
OF COURSE!
ACCORDING TO *THIS* DOCUMENTATION HERE.
WHERE?!
IN WINTER, THE CLIMBING OF SNOWY MOUNTAINS. IN SUMMER, THE ACCEPTING OF DARES. SHARING EXPERIENCES OF *INTENSE* FEAR CAUSES THE LOVE BETWEEN TWO HUMANS TO *BURN* WITH A NEW *PASSION*!!
I AM *MOST* EAGER TO ATTEMPT THIS EXPERIMENT WITH YOU.

BOUND TOGETHER BY YOUR FEAR OF THE DARK, THE LOVE BETWEEN THE THREE OF YOU WILL MOVE UP TO THE NEXT LEVEL!
AAARGH! NOOOOOO!
WHAT DOES HE MEAN BY "NEXT LEVEL" ANYWAY?!
BATHUMP
THIS IS MY L-L-LOVE LIFE WE'RE TALKING ABOUT HERE. I DON'T WANT IT TO BE... PLANNED OUT AS SOME EXPERIMENT.
BATHUMP
I WANT TO MAKE MY OWN DE-DECISIONS ABOUT MY OWN LIFE.
BATHUMP
BATHUMP
BATHUMP
ばあん
BOO

EEK!
SWP
YAA!
tmp
AFH!
AAAHHH!

KYAAAAAAAAAAAAAA
HAZUMU-KUN?!
HAZUMU!!

HM... THAT METHOD FAILED...
shf shf shf shf
TWITCH
Unfortunate.
tptptptp

HAZUMU!!
HAZUMU-
KUN!

KYAAAAAAA!
?

HAZUMU?!
AWESOME! I'M HERE FOR YOU, HAZUMU! COME, RUN INTO MY ARMS!
Come, darling!
OH, ASUTA!

AAAARGH!
POOOW
NICE... KOFF... PUNCH...☆ I KNEW I WAS FRIENDS WITH YOU FOR A REASON...
AHHH!!
THMP THMP THMP THMP
HUFF
HUFF
HUFF
HUFF
HU...
..........!!!

....
SQUISH

A-
AYUKI-CHAN...?

TOUCHING...
SOMETHING LIKE THAT.
IT'S SOMETHING PEOPLE ENJOY...
WHEN IT'S DONE WITH SOMEONE THEY LIKE, CORRECT?
YOU STARTLED ME...
ACK!
SORRY!
UM....
AYUKI-CHAN...?
ABOUT WHAT YOU SAID...
YOU KNOW, "NOT TRYING" AND ALL...
YES?
WHAT DID YOU MEAN?

ARE YOU "TRYING," HAZUMU-KUN?
ER...
UH...
chuckle
IT'S OKAY. THERE'S NOTHING WRONG WITH TRYING.
SO YOU'VE DECLARED WAR ON YASUNA, THEN?
YEAH... PRETTY MUCH...
I THINK THAT'S WHAT LOVE IS ALL ABOUT.
I WANT TO GET ON THE SAME FIELD AS HER AS FAST AS I CAN.
BUT I DON'T INTEND TO STAND ON THE STAGE WITH EVERYONE ELSE.
I'M HAPPY HERE IN THE AUDIENCE...
JUST WATCHING.
JUST WATCHING...?
WHEN I WAS VERY LITTLE...

...I USED TO *LOVE* WATCHING CATERPILLARS LEAVE THEIR CHRYSALLIS AND TURN INTO BUTTERFLIES.

THE JUST-BORN WINGS WERE *STILL* PEARLY WHITE...

AND SO FRAGILE THAT ANY STRAIN WOULD TEAR THEM.

SLOWLY AND PAINFULLY, THEY'D SPREAD THEIR WINGS...

AND LET THEM GRADUALLY DRY INTO BEAUTIFUL, BRIGHT PATTERNS.

I JUST WANTED TO WATCH.

THAT BY ITSELF IS ***ENOUGH*** FOR ME.

BUT I ***NEVER*** ONCE THOUGHT THAT I WOULD WANT TO TRANS-FORM LIKE A BUTTERFLY...

OR DANCE THROUGH THE SKY ON MY OWN COLORFUL WINGS.

I LIKE JUST WATCHING.
OR WOULD YOU RATHER STAY HERE ALONE IN THE BIO LAB?
snicker
THAT'S ITS OWN VARIETY OF LOVE, DON'T YOU THINK?
WELL THEN, LET'S GO.
YEEP!
NOOO!
......
HAZUMU-KUN...
Hazumu-kun!
Hazumu!
Hazumu!

DON'T HURRY YOURSELF. TAKE YOUR TIME IN CHOOSING BETWEEN YASUNA AND TOMARI.
SLOWLY AND CARE-FULLY, SO THAT YOU DON'T TEAR YOUR NEWBORN WINGS.

HOW INTRIGUING.
THERE IS MUCH MORE TO THIS...
THAN IT WOULD APPEAR AT FIRST GLANCE.
SENSEI?!
SORA-SENSEI!!

WHERE ARE YO--?!
WHAAA?!
HAZU-MUUU!! I'LL SAVE YOUUU!!
THUD
WHUMP
CRASH
......
Let's go home.
Yeah, let's.

HAZUMU-KUN...

#11 The Princess of Curry

BUT...

AH!

#11 The Princess of Curry

IT'S KINDA BRIGHT HERE...
BUT STILL! EATING OUTSIDE MAKES LUNCH TASTE LOADS BETTER, DON'T YOU THINK?
OH, NEAT! TOMARI-CHAN, YOUR LUNCH LOOKS SO YUMMY!
WANNA TRADE FOR SOME OF MY MEAT-BALLS?
....
Who-ever else wants some can have some!

YASUNA-CHAN?
YASUNA-CHAN...?
OH... YES?
DO YOU WANT SOME MEATBALLS?
SURE.
I WILL TAKE SOME.
Yum! Thanks!
You can have some of my vege-tables.

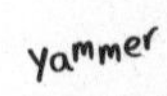
Yammer

Yammer
......

BIIIING
BOOONG
BEEEENG
THERE SHE IS...

HAZUMU-KUN!
YIKES!
OH...!
I'M SO SORRY... I SURPRISED YOU AGAIN, DIDN'T I...?
N-NO... IT'S OKAY.
WHAT'S UP?
UM...
WHAT DO YOU HAVE IN THE BASKET?
HM?
THESE?

THEY'RE SOME OF THE VEGETABLES MY CLUB RAISED!
CARROTS, POTATOES AND ONIONS!
HOW WONDERFUL! I DIDN'T KNOW THE GARDENING CLUB ALSO DID VEGATABLES.
WELL, "GARDENING CLUB" IS JUST OUR OFFICIAL NAME. IN REALITY, WE'RE MORE OF A HORTICULTURE CLUB.
WE DO JUST ABOUT ANY-THING THAT INVOLVES PLANTS.

CARROTS... POTATOES...
HA HA! YEP! AND THEY'RE ALSO THE INGREDI-ENTS FOR CURRY!
DO YOU WANT TO TAKE SOME HOME?

CURRY?
HMM... NOW THAT'S AN IDEA...

HAZUMU-KUN...
HOW ABOUT WE TAKE ALL OF THESE AND HOLD A CURRY-PARTY AT MY HOUSE?

HUH?

INTRIGUING.
COOKING, HM?
AND YOUR FIRST INVITATION TO HER HOUSE!!
ZWSH
WE'RE ALL GOING, NOT JUST ME!
HM. IT IS HIGHLY POSSIBLE FOR THE CULINARY ARTS TO HAVE SIMILARITIES WITH "LOVE."
He's getting ideas again, isn't he?
THE JOY OF COOKING.
THE JOY OF EATING.
THE JOY OF LOVE.
THE JOY OF LIVING.
CONSEQUENTLY, THOSE BEINGS WHO DISCARD ALL FEELINGS OF JOY IN FAVOR OF A COLDLY CLINICAL MINDSET...
ARE LEFT WITH NO CHOICE BUT TO WALK THE ROAD TO RUIN.

JAN-PUU LOVES CURRY!
MAMA-SAMA MADE MILD CURRY! IT WAS SUPER PUUMMY! ♡
YEAH. DO YOU WANT TO GO WITH US?
PUUUUU! ♡
PUUU-♥

WOULD YOU LIKE TO COME TOO...?
OF COURSE.

ピンポーン
DINGDONG
WHY, HELLO THERE.

OH, THIS MUST BE THE COUSIN YOU TOLD ME ABOUT YESTERDAY...
UH... H-HI.

YOU'RE JAN-PUU-CHAN, CORRECT?
WEL-COME.
And Sensei, of course.
PUUUU!
YASUNAN!

STILL, A SUDDEN INVITATION FOR ALL OF US TO YASUNA'S HOUSE? SHE MUST HAVE SOMETHING PLANNED...
WHAT THE HELL ARE YOU TALKING ABOUT?
--AHA! THERE IT IS! KAMIIZUMI.
DUDE, IT'S HUGE!
DING DONG
YES?
SHOULD BE AROUND HERE SOME-WHERE...
SORRY TO INTRUDE...
COME IN, COME IN.
MY PARENTS ARE AWAY THIS WEEKEND, SO PLEASE FEEL FREE TO MAKE YOURSELF AT HOME.
WHAT?!
"THERE'S NOBODY HOME TODAY"...?
rrrg
WUMP

?
UM... MY NAME IS KURUSU, WE WERE INVITED...
AH!
TOMARI-CHAN?
HAZUMU?!
YOU'RE HERE ALREADY?
YEP!
I'LL GET THE DOOR! JUST A SEC!
?
COME IN!
K-CHIK
WELCOME, WELCOME!
WE'VE BEEN WAITING FOR YOU!
--OH, WAIT. THIS ISN'T MY HOUSE. OOPS.
tee hee
HAZU--!
THAT LOOKS SCARILY GOOD ON YOU...
A-A-A-APR--APRON?!!

DARLING! ♡
WELCOME HOME! YOU MUST BE SO TIRED. ♡
WHICH WOULD YOU LIKE FIRST? A BATH... DINNER...
OR PERHAPS...?
ME?

HELLO, ALL! YOU'RE QUITE LATE!
GYAAAAA
HURG

WE HAVE ALREADY BEGUN COOKING. COME IN AND HELP.
YEEEEEEEEEEEEEEE
SENSEI!
WAAAAAAA
SENSEI, PLEASE! DON'T TURN AROUND!!

SORA-SENSEI!?!

DRAT... JUST A DREAM.
SIGH. IT'S A *WONDERFULLY* BEAUTIFUL SUNDAY...
YET HERE I SIT, ALL BY MY LONESOME, WATCHING TV AND EATING A MICROWAVE DINNER.
HOW TERRIBLY LONELY...
I'D RATHER SPEND A *GORGEOUS* DAY LIKE THIS...
ON A DATE WITH MY *PRECIOUS* SORA-SENSEI!
AAAH, SENSEI...
JAM
HOP
HOP
NGA?!

Well, how about this, then?
Too out of date.
WOW, IS IT JUST ME, OR DOES THAT SMELL *REALLY* GOOD?
ONEE-NII-SAMA!
LET'S KEEP COOKING!
YASUNAN IS *SO* AMAZING! ♡
SHE'S REALLY, REALLY, REALLY, *REALLY* GOOD AT COOKING!
Ah! Tomarin! Hello!!
twitch
GOOD AT COOKING ...?
I'VE BEEN TOTALLY *USELESS* THE WHOLE TIME.
TOMARI-CHAN, TAKE OVER FOR ME. PLEASE?
HUH?! ER... UH... SURE.

HELLO.
I'M SORRY I COULDN'T COME GREET YOU. I COULDN'T LET THIS BURN.
HAS EVERYONE ARRIVED?
YEP.
FEEL FREE TO USE ANYTHING YOU FIND. I DON'T MIND.
LET'S GET CRACKIN' THEN!
WE'LL START OVER HERE.
TOMARI...?
IF YOU TAKE THE MEAT AND SOAK IT IN RED WINE OVERNIGHT...
AND *LIGHTLY* SEAR IT BEFORE PUTTING IT IN TO COOK...

...IT TURNS OUT TO BE *VERY* DELICIOUS.
WOW~!
MAYBE I SHOULD HAVE GOTTEN A LITTLE MORE MEAT...?
WHY NOT USE *THIS*?
NO! THANK YOU!
UM... THIS IS *CURRY*, RIGHT?
I THOUGHT YOU JUST FOLLOWED THE INSTRUCTIONS ON THE BACK OF THE BOX...
OH MY GOSH! YASUNA-CHAN, THAT'S SO AMAZING!
YOU'RE EVEN MIXING THE *SPICES* FROM SCRATCH!!

HEY, ASUTA? ABOUT YASUNA...
HM?
SHE'S REALLY... FEMININE, YOU KNOW?
GUYS LIKE HER TYPE...
INSTEAD OF... OTHERS, DON'T THEY?
REALLY? I DUNNO...
PERSONALLY, BETWEEN THE TWO OF THEM, I'D TAKE HAZUM--
VRK
Shake Shake
PLOP
PLOP
PLOP
CHOP

CRUMBLE
CRUMBLE

AYUKI, WHY DON'T YOU DO THIS AFTER ALL...?
REALLY?! CAN I?
TOMARI! IF YOU VALUE YOUR LIFE, DO IT YOURSELF!!

ONEE-NII-SAMA! COULD YOU HELP JAN-PUU WITH THIS, *PWEEEASE?*
COMING!
......
HERE. LET ME HELP.
HUH...?
......
SHK SHK

YASUNA...
WHY?
WHY INVITE ME AND THE OTHERS?
WHAT ...?
WHY NOT *JUST* HAZUMU?
AT FIRST...
I INTENDED TO DO *JUST* THAT.
I MEAN, YOU WOULD'VE BEEN *HAPPIER* IF IT WAS JUST YOU AND HER, RIGHT? SO WHY?
BUT...
Jan-puu-chan, get that corner over there, 'kay?

THE HAZUMU-KUN WHO...
TALKS TO HER FAVORITE PLANTS...
IS SUCH A FRAIDY-CAT.
SHE LOOKS AT ME LIKE SHE'S UNSURE OF WHAT TO DO.
THEY ARE ALL **WONDERFUL**... BUT THERE IS ANOTHER *DIFFERENT* HAZUMU-KUN...
HAZUMU-KUN'S BIGGEST, BRIGHTEST SMILE...

IS SOMETHING SHE ONLY SHARES WHEN **EVERYONE** IS TOGETHER.
ONE THAT I WILL NEVER, EVER SEE BY MYSELF.

I WANT ALL OF HAZUMU-KUN.
I WANT HER TO SMILE THAT SMILE FOR ME.
I *CERTAINLY* DON'T WANT TO GIVE HER UP TO YOU, KURUSU-SAN!
I WANT TO MAKE HER *MINE*, KEEP HER ALL TO MYSELF...
BUT NOT RIGHT NOW.
FOR NOW, I JUST WANT TO WATCH OVER HER.

YOU, WHO ARE MORE PRECIOUS TO ME THAN ANYTHING...
AND YOUR WONDERFUL, BRILLIANT SMILE.
"TOMARI."
HMM?
CALL ME "TOMARI."
IT'S ONLY FAIR. I'VE ALWAYS CALLED YOU BY YOUR FIRST NAME.

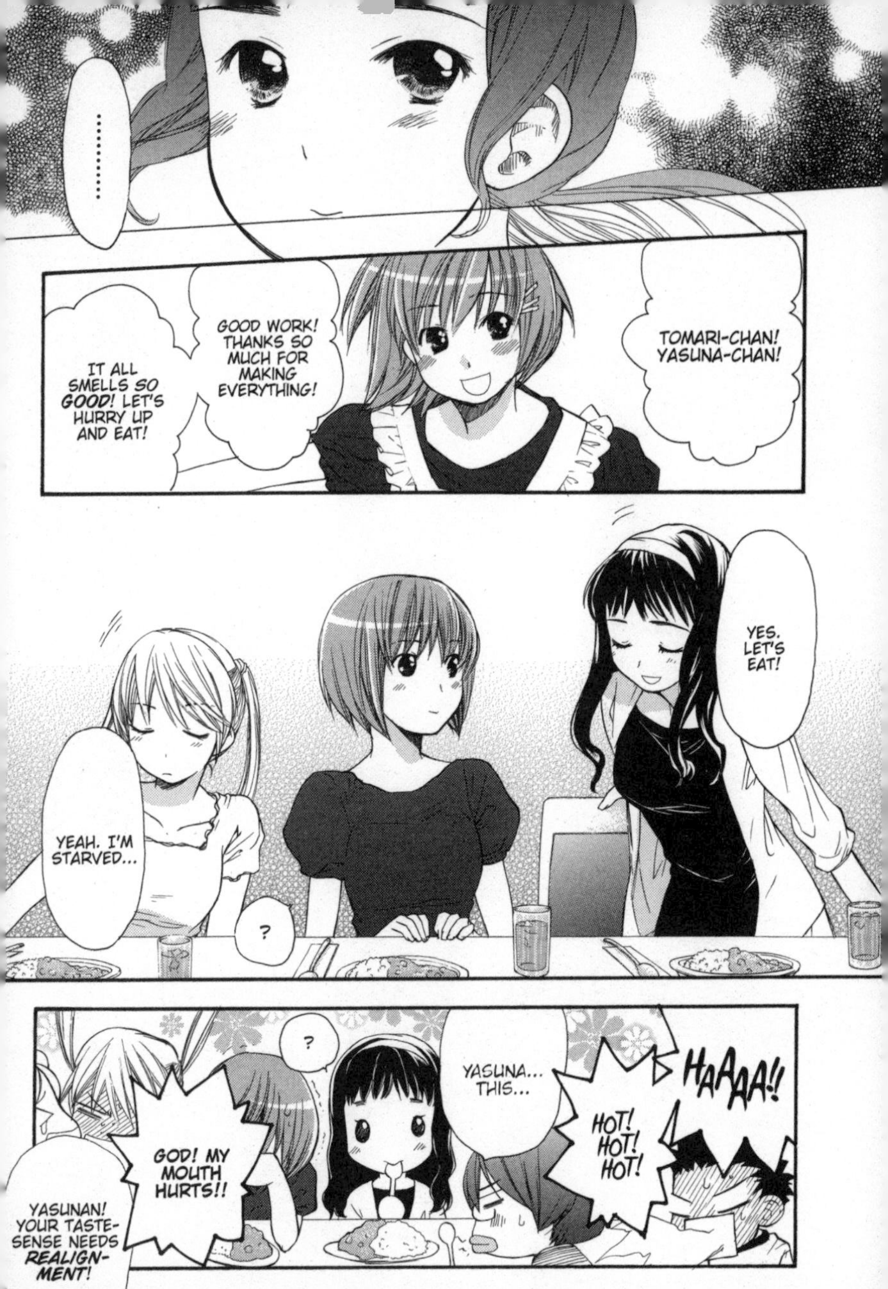
....
TOMARI-CHAN! YASUNA-CHAN!
GOOD WORK! THANKS SO MUCH FOR MAKING EVERYTHING!
IT ALL SMELLS SO *GOOD*! LET'S HURRY UP AND EAT!
YES. LET'S EAT!
?
YEAH. I'M STARVED...
HAAAA!!
HOT! HOT! HOT!
YASUNA... THIS...
?
GOD! MY MOUTH HURTS!!
YASUNAN! YOUR TASTE-SENSE NEEDS ***REALIGNMENT***!

#12 Of Summer Festivals and Cotton Candy

Toast with bacon and eggs.

INTRIGUING... "SUMMER FESTIVAL," HM...?
ZIIIING
"SHINTO SHRINE." "LOVE."
TK
TK
TK
CRAP!
He's getting another one of THOSE ideas!
NOOKIE IN THE DARK BEHIND THE SHRINE?!
yeah, right!
OH? WHY NOT? THERE ARE BEINGS WITH JUST SUCH AN EXPERIENCE IN THIS VERY ROOM, AFTER ALL.
HUH?!
RUFFLE

WHAT IS THE PROBLEM? ARE NOT HUMAN OFFSPRING EXPECTED TO CONTINUE THE FAMILY TRADITION?
nookie
nookie
WHAT "TRADITION"?!
KOFF
KOFF
AHEM... WELL... URM... SPEAKING OF THE SUMMER FESTIVAL, WHEN YOU WERE STILL LITTLE, THERE WAS A TIME WHEN YOUR MOM BROUGHT YOU HOME, CRYING.
HUH?

SHE DID? HMM...
OH YEAH, I REMEMBER NOW, SORTA.
THERE WAS ONE THING I WAS STUCK ON, SOMETHING I KEPT REPEATING OVER AND OVER...
BUT I CAN'T REMEMBER WHAT IT--
...NDY...!
...TTON... AN...
WHAT THE HECK?
WHAT WAS IT?
EVERYBODY'S GOING TO THE FESTIVAL TONIGHT, RIGHT?
THE ONE AT KASHIMA SHRINE? YOU BET!
THIS YEAR, I'LL PICK THE RIGHT ONE FOR SURE!
"PICK THE RIGHT ONE"?

YEAH. ONE OF KASHIMA SHRINE'S OLD FESTIVAL TRADITIONS.
IT'S PRETTY SIMPLE, REALLY.
THERE'LL BE *TWO* UPSIDE-DOWN BOWLS.
UNDER *ONE* OF THEM IS A PIECE OF CANDY.
YOU GUESS THE RIGHT BOWL, AND THE SHRINE *KAMI* WILL GRANT YOUR WISH.
PLUS, YOU GET TO KEEP THE CANDY.
WOW. HOW INTER-ESTING.
I *REALLY* STINK AT IT. I MESS UP *EVERY* YEAR.
I GET SO NERVOUS... I CAN'T PICK *EITHER* ONE...
HEY, IT'S ALL JUST LUCK. DON'T LET IT GET YOU DOWN.
YEAH, I KNOW. BUT...
...NDY...!
...TTON... AN...
--THERE IT IS AGAIN.
WHERE HAVE I HEARD THAT BEFORE, ANYWAY?

OF COURSE, EVERYONE WILL WEAR *YUKATAS* TONIGHT, RIGHT?
CLAP
CLAP
HUH?
WHA?!
I CAN'T WAIT TO SEE THE YUKATA YOU'LL WEAR, HAZUMU-KUN.
BUT I DON'T THINK I HAVE A YUKATA...
NO. WAIT. I'M SURE I DO.
......
BONK
WHAT I WANT TO KNOW IS WHAT KIND OF YUKATA *TOMARI* WILL WEAR.
HEY!!

YEAH! COME ON, TOMARI-CHAN!
WEAR A YUKATA WITH THE REST OF US!
HUH?!
I...
I...
DON'T REALLY HAVE--
I KNOW! WHY DON'T WE WEAR THE SAME COLOR?!
HAZUMU-KUN IS SURE TO LOOK CUTE IN ANY COLOR!
REALLY ...?
I don't think so...
YASUNA WOULD LOOK GOOD IN ANY COLOR TOO.
....
THMP
THMP
THMP

WHAAAAM
MOM!!
OH... WELCOME HOME, TOMARI.
COULD YOU BUY ME A YUKATA?! FOR, LIKE, TONIGHT?!!
SILENCE...
HUFF
HUFF
......?
OH MY GOD! MOM, ONEECHAN'S GONE INSANE!
S-SEKIHAN! TONIGHT, WE'LL HAVE SEKIHAN!!
KNOCK IT OFF!!!

HAZUMU IN A YUKATA...
puff
puff
A DATE WITH HAZUMU IN A YUKATA...
In your dreams!
OH, DEAR!
I WONDER WHICH ONE SORA-SENSEI WOULD LIKE BEST? THIS ONE? OR THAT ONE?
I CAN HARDLY DECIDE WHICH ONE TO WEAR!
SENSEI...
A DATE WITH SORA-SENSEI... IN YUKATAS...

GOOD EVENING.
NAMIKO, YOU LOOK STUNNINGLY GORGEOUS IN THAT YUKATA.
HITOSHI-SAN...
SO MUCH SO...
THAT I WANT TO SPIN YOU LIKE A TOP!!
KYAAAHH?!
SWOOSH
HA HA HA! ISN'T THIS ENTER-TAINING?
AHH, HITOSHI-SAN!
AAHN!
WEEEN!
SWUP
SWUP
THUUUD...

SOMETHING REALLY SAD HAD JUST HAPPENED.

WOW!
THERE ARE SO MANY STANDS!
WELL, YEAH... THIS IS A FESTIVAL AFTER ALL.
Jeez, they look so alike when they spaz.
OH MY GOD! WHERE SHOULD WE START? HERE? MAYBE THERE?
OH, TOMARI-CHAN. WHAT'S WRONG?
fidget
fidget
N-NOTHING...
I JUST... DIDN'T HAVE A YUKATA, SO I KINDA GOT STUCK WEARING ONE OF MY MOM'S OLD ONES...
AND IT'S SO TIGHT AND IT FEELS WEIRD AND IT'S HARD TO WALK IN...

JUST LIKE I FIGURED...
YASUNA LOOKS PERFECT IN A YUKATA.
?
WHY?
YOU LOOK SO *CUTE* IN IT.
HUH?
blush
UH...
?
steam steam
UM... AHH...
TOMARI-CHAN?

HEY, MISTER!
TAKE THIS!
UH?!
TOMARI SUPER SPECIAL ATTACK!
SPLISH SPLISH SPLISH SPLISH
HERE.
huff
huff
ONEE-NII-SAMA? WHAT'S THAT POOFY THING THERE? IT'S CUTE!
AH! COTTON CANDY! I COULD REALLY GO FOR SOME RIGHT NOW.
SHOULD I GET THE PINK ONE OR THE WHITE ONE?
OH... UH, THANKS...
I DON'T KNOW WHICH OF THEM IS HAPPIER...
HUH...?
PINK OR... WHITE...?

AH...
THIS AGAIN.
WHY ON EARTH DOES IT KEEP COMING TO MIND...?
HAZUMU!
HAZUMU-KUN!
SNAP!!
I SAW SOME CANDY APPLES OVER THERE.
YOU WANT TO GO GET SOME *TAKOYAKI*?
UH...

WELL...
UHH...
I...
I HAVE TO GO TO THE BATHROOM!!
RUN
WHA...?
....
HFF
HFF
THIS *ALWAYS* HAPPENS...
hff
hff
I ALWAYS END UP JUST RUNNING AWAY...
EVEN THOUGH I KNOW...
THAT'S THE *WORST* THING I COULD DO.

YEEP!
W-W-WHAT THE HECK ARE YOU DOING OUT HERE?!
Especially in THAT outfit!!
SHH! RELAX. I AM VISIBLE ONLY TO YOU. AS FOR YOUR QUESTION...
I AM IN THE MIDST OF AN OBSER-VATION.
AN OBSER-VATION ...?

TEE HEE
Oooh
MAKIN' OUT
........!!!

P-P-P-PEEPING IS A CRIME!!!
IT IS...?
OH WELL. NEVER-MIND THAT. WHAT IS WRONG?
YOUR EMOTIONAL STATE APPEARS ***UNBAL-ANCED***.

PLOP
WHAT'S THIS?
HRM.
I... UM... WELL...
I COULDN'T CHOOSE. I'VE ALWAYS BEEN PRETTY INDECISIVE...
A MEMORY...
FROM WHEN I WAS LITTLE.
COME ON, HAZUMU. WHICH ONE DO YOU WANT?

BOTH!
NO, PICK ONE.
IT HAS TO BE ONE OR THE OTHER.
PINK OR WHITE...
WHITE OR PINK...
OH NO! RAIN!
COME ON, HAZUMU! WE'RE GOING HOME!
WAAAAH! BUT I WANT COTTON CANDY!
IF YOU'D MADE UP YOUR MIND FASTER, YOU COULD'VE HAD SOME!
GOODNESS, SUCH A SILLY CHILD...
IF YOU DON'T LEARN HOW TO CHOOSE, IT'S GOING TO GET YOU IN TROUBLE SOMEDAY. AND BOY, ARE YOU GOING TO REGRET IT THEN!

OH...
THAT'S RIGHT.
I CRIED ALL NIGHT...
AFTER A WHILE, I JUST STARTED GIVING UP. I'D RUN AWAY...
BUT I NEVER DID GET ANY BETTER ABOUT DECISIONS.
I'VE NEVER BEEN ABLE TO CHOOSE, AND I ALWAYS END UP REGRETTING IT.
TRYING MY BEST TO FORGET ALL ABOUT IT AND WAIT FOR ALL THE FUSS TO DIE DOWN.
IF THINGS KEEP GOING THE WAY THEY ARE...
THEN SOMEDAY I'M GOING TO HAVE TO--
SHUDDER
BUT I DON'T WANT TO GIVE UP.
NOT THIS TIME.

BUT...

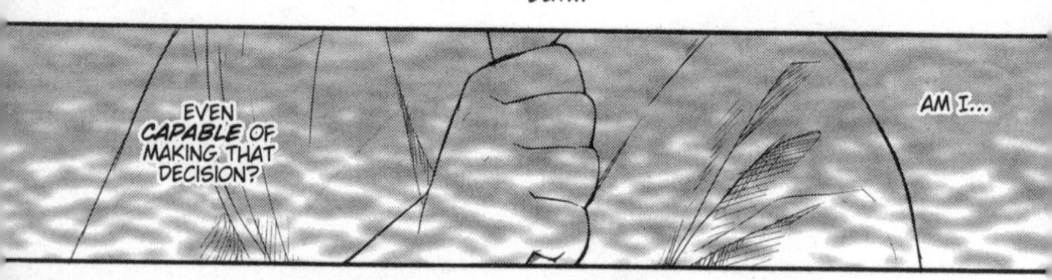

I STILL DON'T *EVEN* KNOW WHAT LOVE REALLY IS.

OR IS IT SOMETHING ELSE ENTIRELY...?
GO AHEAD.
O-OKAY...
UMM...
UHHH...
wiffle
wiffle
DANG IT! HERE GOES! I WISH I WASN'T SO INDECI-SIVE!
GRAB

HA!
UH...?
I'M SORRY.
AW, MAN~!
SIGH...
SO I'M NOT GOING TO FIX MY INDECI-SIVENESS THIS YEAR EITHER... DRAT.
とぼ PLOD
とぼ PLOD
HAZUMU!
HERE, HAZUMU-KUN! I BOUGHT SOME FOR YOU.
YOU WANTED COTTON CANDY, RIGHT? HERE.
HUH?

UH...
UMM...
TH-THANKS...
BOTH OF YOU...
SMILE
SO SWEET...
GOD...
ARE YOU TRYING TO TELL ME THAT THINGS WILL BE OKAY THE WAY THEY ARE...?
FOR JUST A LITTLE WHILE LONGER AT LEAST...
RIGHT...?
GOD...?
わたがし
500

#13 A Little Storm

Would you like one?
......
SEASIDE PARK
WELL, THAT DOES IT FOR THE FIRST SEMESTER.
NOW IT'S *FINALLY* SUMMER VACATION!
DON'T YOU HAVE SUMMER SCHOOL THIS YEAR?
URK!

DON'T WORRY, ASUTA. I'VE STILL GOT TO COME FOR CLUB, SO YOU WON'T BE *ALL* ALONE.
HA MU
OH? SO YOU'RE BUSY THIS SUMMER, THEN?
NO, NOT REALLY. IT'S NOT LIKE I HAVE TO COME EVERY DAY.
whew
OH. THAT'S GOOD...
......
YAAAAA
ka ka ka ka ka ka
heh heh heh
SAY, EVERYONE...!
WHY DON'T WE ALL VISIT THIS PLACE SOMETIME?
SEASIDE PARK

SEASIDE PARK
AN AQUARIUM?
ONE THAT'S BEEN MESHED WITH AN AMUSEMENT PARK, ACCORDING TO THE FLYER.
OH YEAH! I'VE SEEN *THIS* BEFORE! IT WAS ON TV.
SURE, I'LL GO!
WHAT?! THEY'RE GIVING AWAY MARIN-CHAN CELLPHONE STRAPS TO THE FIRST VISITORS ON OPENING DAY?!
I SOOO WANT ONE!
SO, LET'S GO THEN.
OPENING DAY IS THE DAY AFTER TOMORROW.
AWESOME!
YOU'RE COMING TOO, RIGHT, ASUTA?
CAN'T. SUMMER CLASSES START THAT DAY.
OH WELL. NO BIG LOSS.
NOW THAT'S JUST CRUEL!!

I'LL BUY YOU SOMETHING FROM THE GIFT SHOP.
tee hee
FRIENDSHIP
HAZUMUUU!

WE CAN TURN IT INTO A GIRLS' DAY OUT.
WOO HOO!
heh heh
?
HAZUMUUU...
....

I CAN'T ***WAIT***! HOW ABOUT YOU, TOMARI-CHAN?

TOMARI-CHAN?
HUH?
OH. YEAH, RIGHT. CAN'T WAIT.

BEAM BEAM
TOMARI?
?
DID YOU GET THE SUMMER TRAINING CAMP SCHEDULE?
YEAH, I GOT IT.
GOD... COACH DOESN'T KNOW THE MEANING OF THE WORD "MERCY."
DON'T FORGET TO BE HERE BY FIVE AM ON THE FIRST DAY!
RIGHT.
DON'T BE LATE, 'KAY?!
I HEAR YA.

THAT'S THE DAY *AFTER* TOMORROW, GOT IT?!
HA HA...
LOOKS LIKE MY SUMMER VACATION ISN'T STARTING UNTIL TRAINING CAMP IS OVER.
OH...
AH...
DONE WITH ENSEMBLE?
YES. WHAT ABOUT YOU, KURUSU-SAN?
YOU CAN CALL ME "TOMARI," REMEMBER...?
OH! THAT'S RIGHT.

UM... TOMARI-SAN...?

HN.

I HOPE WE HAVE FUN TOGETHER ON OUR TRIP...

HN?

OUR TRIP THE DAY AFTER TOMORROW. REMEMBER?

HUH?

WHA~~?!!

YOU CAN'T COOOME?!
boo...
Aww, why not?! Come on!
HAZUMUU!
SOMEBODY EXPLAIN TO ME WHY HER REACTION IS SO DIFFERENT FROM WHEN I SAID I COULDN'T COME!

I DON'T HAVE MUCH OF A CHOICE... IT'S A FIVE-DAY OVERNIGHT CAMP.
God, is it ever going to be harsh...
THAT'S SOOOO UNFAIR!
THMPA
THMPA
WELL, YOU REALLY WANT THAT CELLPHONE STRAP, RIGHT?
JUST GO ON WITHOUT ME. I DON'T MIND.
OH... OKAY...
BUT WHEN YOU GET BACK, WE'LL HAVE TO GO AGAIN... TOGETHER!

SIGH...
FIVE WHOLE DAYS WITHOUT TOMARI-CHAN.
IT'S GOING TO BE SO LONELY...
HUH?!
BATHUMP
twitch
H-HAZUMU...!
DON'T TELL ME YOU'RE GETTING STARTED ON THAT AGAIN...?!
JUST KIDDING!
DON'T WORRY, I'LL BE FINE. I'M NOT A LITTLE KID ANYMORE.
SO DO YOUR BEST AT THE TRAINING CAMP, OKAY?

Y-YEAH... OKAY...
....
I'm so dead!
ouch
IT'S BEEN AGES...
SINCE I LAST...
WALKED HOME BY MYSELF...

TOMARI-CHA--
....
な屋
堂書店

……
ONEE-NII-SAMA!
WHOA!
JAN-PUU-CHAN, WHAT'S WRONG?
nuzzle nuzzle
JAN-PUU DOESN'T WANT TO GO! JAN-PUU DOESN'T WANT TO LEAVE ONEE-NII-SAMA!!
IT IS NECESSARY FOR ROUTINE MAINTENANCE THAT I RESTORE JAN-PUU TO HER TRUE FORM FOR APPROXIMATELY THREE DAYS.
HER "*TRUE* FORM." YOU MEAN THE SPACE SHIP?
CORRECT.
IT'S OKAY, JAN-PUU-CHAN. IT'S NOT LIKE YOU'LL ***NEVER*** SEE ME AGAIN.
WAAAAAH! EVEN IF IT IS ONLY THREE DAYS, JAN-PUU STILL DOESN'T WANT TO LEAVE ONEE-NII-SAMA!!!

IT'S GOOD THAT YOU CAN SAY WHAT YOU FEEL, JAN-PUU-CHAN...
there there
PUU?
"IT'S GOING TO BE SO LONELY..."
FIRST SHE GOES AND SAYS SOMETHING LIKE *THAT*...
AND THEN SHE JUST LETS ME GO WITHOUT A FUSS?
IT MAKES ME WONDER...
BRRRRRNG

HM...? FROM AYUKI?
brrrng
WHAT COULD SHE WANT?
PI
WHAT?!
"SORRY."
"SOMETHING CAME UP."
BRRRRNG

"HAZUMU-KUN IS GOING TO BE LEFT ALONE WITH YASUNA!"
"FORGIVE ME!"
....
SQUEEZE
....

YEESH.
SNAP
LOOKS LIKE IT'S DOWN TO JUST THE **TWO** OF US NOW...
I GUESS... WE'LL HAVE TO DO THIS SOME OTHER DAY, THEN.
GLOOM
HUH?
OH! NO NO NO! IT'S **OKAY**. TODAY'S FINE!
SEE!
WE GOT THE CELLPHONE STRAP AND EVERYTHING. MIGHT AS WELL STAY!
OH...!
WE BOTH HAVE THE **SAME** ONE...

COME ON, YASUNA-CHAN! LET'S GO HAVE SOME FUN!
I'M SORRY...
BUT JUST FOR TODAY, I'M GOING TO KEEP YOU ALL TO MYSELF.

TOMARI-CHAN...
SHE WAS LAUGHING.
SHE LOOKED LIKE SHE WAS HAVING LOADS OF FUN...
EVEN THOUGH I WASN'T THERE.
HAZUMU-KUN.
I'M SORRY I KEPT YOU WAITING.

ARE YOU FEELING A LITTLE TIRED?
HUH...?
OH... UH, NO... NOT REALLY.

SHALL WE GO FOR A RIDE ON THE FERRIS WHEEL...?
KLANK
RATTLE

PENNY FOR YOUR THOUGHTS?
OH... UH...
IT'S NOTHING, REALLY. I WAS JUST FEELING A LITTLE *GUILTY* THAT THE TWO OF US ARE HERE HAVING FUN WITHOUT ANY OF THE OTHERS.
HUH?

PI
PI
PI
AM I... NOT GOOD ENOUGH...?
HUH...?
WHAT DID YOU SAY?
ARE YOU LONELY WITHOUT TOMARI-SAN?
--HUH?
HAZUMU-KUN...
DO YOU REALLY--

ACK!
OH!
BRRRRRNG
IT'S JUST MY PHONE.
BRRRRRNG
BRRRRRNG
BRRRRRNG
BRRRRRNG
AH...
BRRRRRNG
IT'S TOMARI-CHAN.
SWAP
NO!

BRRRRRNG
BRRRRRNG
PLEASE...!
BRRRRNG
DON'T ANSWER IT...
BRRRRNG
BRRRRRNG
来栖とまり
KURUSU Tomari

BRRRRNG
BRRRRNG
YASUNA-CHAN...
BRRRRN

BRRRRRNG
ルルルッ...
BRRRRNG
......
......
ERK
SILENCE...

SMILE
ニコ...
DO YOU MIND IF WE STAY LIKE THIS? JUST FOR A LITTLE WHILE LONGER...?
OKAY...
HAZUMU-KUN...
HM?

!
This gondola will soon reach the ground.
WHY DON'T WE JUST GO STRAIGHT HOME FROM HERE?

O-OKAY...

18 : 40
KURUSU, Tomari
来栖とまり
19 : 55
KURUSU, Tomari
来栖とまり
PI
PI
WHY DIDN'T YOU PICK UP?
I COULDN'T POSSIBLY SAY--
NO WAY!
いえ、ないっ
SNAP
FLOP
OH JEEZ! WHAT DO I DO?!
FLOP
WHAT AM I GOING TO SAY WHEN SHE ASKS ME THAT?

YASUNA-CHAN...
SHE'S THE FIRST GIRL I EVER FELL IN LOVE WITH.

SHE WAS ALWAYS SO BEAUTIFUL, SO NICE.
WHEN SHE SMILED, IT WAS LIKE THE BLOOMING OF A FLOWER.

I JUST WANTED TO BE AROUND HER MORE...
TALK WITH HER MORE...
HAVE HER SMILE AT ME MORE...
ドクン
BA
THUMP
I NEVER KNEW...
LIPS COULD BE SO WARM...
BATHUMP
BATHUMP
BATHUMP

BRRRRRRRRRRRRNG
ACK!!
BRRRRRNG
BRRRRRRNG
B-THMP
B-THMP
BATHUMP BATHUMP
BRRRRRNG
AH!
着信
来栖とまり
KURUSU, Tomari
TOMARI-CHAN...
DO I ANSWER IT...?
BRRRRRNG
BRRRRRRRNG
BRRNG...

snap
……
SNAP
WHY THE HELL ISN'T THAT *PUTZ* ANSWERING...?
KURUSU! LIGHTS OUT AND GO TO SLEEP! ***NOW!***
YES, SIR!
不在着信　3件
3 MISSED CALLS

bed-head
I'VE GOT TO APOLOGIZE TO HER...!
I'm so sorry, Tomari-Chan
BUT THERE'S NO WAY I COULD TELL HER THE REASON WHY I DIDN'T ANSWER.
AW, MAN...!
I JUST COULDN'T.
SO... WHAT COULD I TELL HER, THEN? AND OVER THE PHONE, NO LESS...
......
I KNOW!
ばっ
SWSH
FWMP

K-KLAK
K-KLAK

HA!

WELL... I'M HERE.
B-THUMP
B-THUMP

deep breath

FWEEEET
ANOTHER LAP!
SHF SHF

HAZUMU...
WHY WON'T YOU ANSWER YOUR PHONE? SOMETHING BETTER NOT HAVE HAPPENED...
WHEEZE
FWEEP
FOUR MORE SETS!
YES, SIR!!
I'M CALLING 'TIL YOU ANSWER!!
GRAWR
TOMARI... NO RUNNING WITH SILLY FACES, 'KAY?
WHAT DID YOU SAY?!
EEEEEE
Fweeeet

HN?
RUB
THOUGHT I SAW HAZUMU THERE FOR A SEC...

GREAT. I'M EXHAUSTED TO THE POINT OF HALLUCINATING ALREADY...
SLUMP

WOW!
NATURE IS ALWAYS SO BEAUTIFUL.
I DIDN'T REALLY THINK TOO HARD BEFORE I CAME OUT HERE.
I COMPLETELY FORGOT THAT YOU CAN'T GET IN UNLESS YOU'RE ON THE TRACK TEAM.
TOMARI-CHAN...
YASUNA-CHAN...

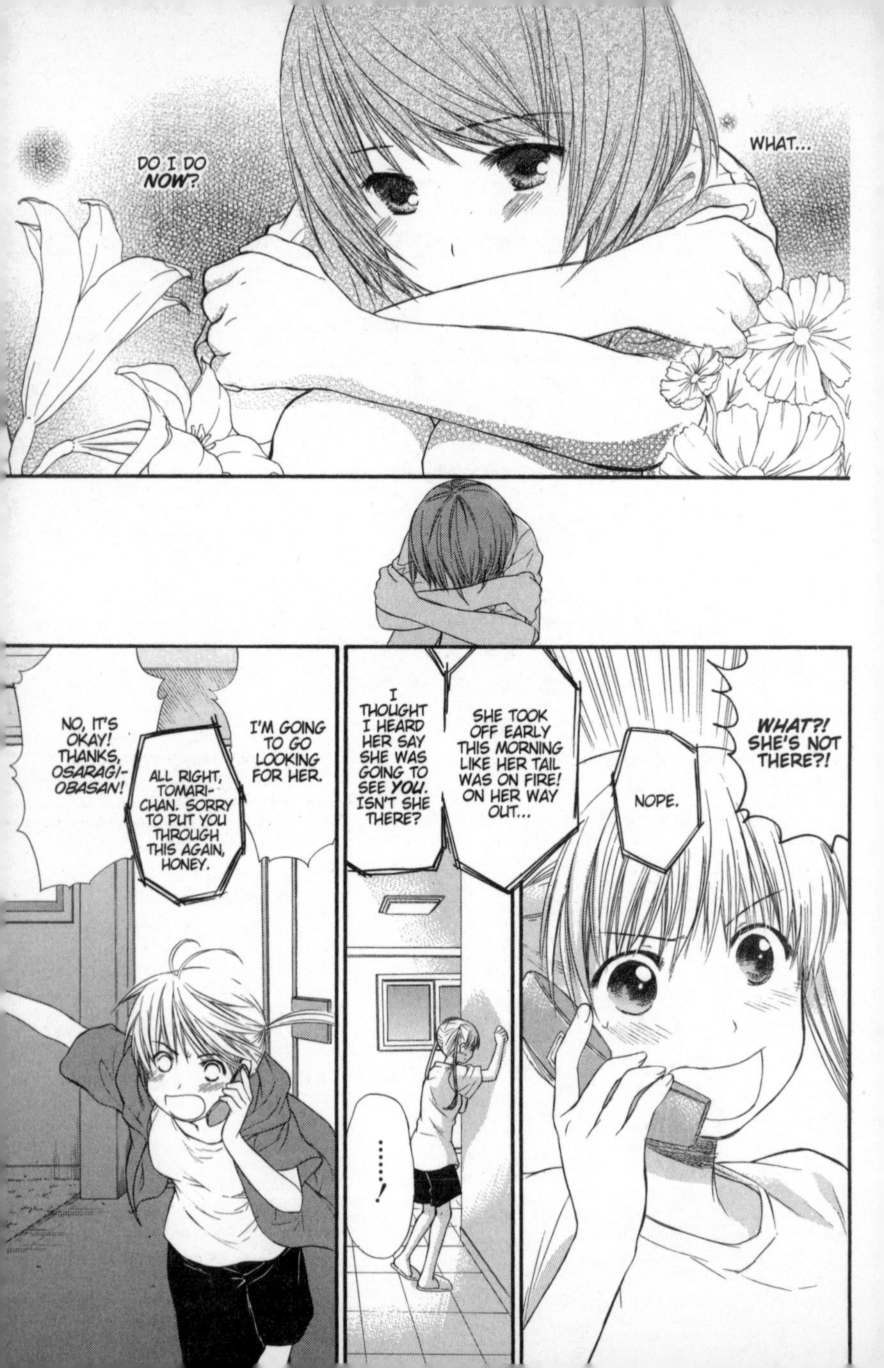
WHAT...
DO I DO *NOW*?
WHAT?! SHE'S NOT THERE?!
NOPE.
SHE TOOK OFF EARLY THIS MORNING LIKE HER TAIL WAS ON FIRE! ON HER WAY OUT...
I THOUGHT I HEARD HER SAY SHE WAS GOING TO SEE *YOU*. ISN'T SHE THERE?
......!
I'M GOING TO GO LOOKING FOR HER.
ALL RIGHT, TOMARI-CHAN. SORRY TO PUT YOU THROUGH THIS AGAIN, HONEY.
NO, IT'S OKAY! THANKS, *OSARAGI-OBASAN!*

UH-OH...
PLUNK
I FELL ASLEEP...
AND...
I LOST MY CELL-PHONE...!
TO--
TOMARI-CHAAAAAN!

PUU! ♥
MAINTENANCE ALL DONE!
Peace!
ONEE-NII-SAMA, I'M HOME!
shiver shiver
JAN-PUU-CHAAAAN!
びええええええん
WAAAAAAAAH
OOH! ONEE-NII-SAMA, YOU'RE SO ENTHUSIASTIC! JAN-PUU IS SO HAPPY!

HAZUMU WAS HERE AFTER ALL!
I EVEN SAW HER... HOW COULD I THINK IT WAS JUST A HALLUCINATION? STUPID!!
BRRRNG
BRRRNG
HAZUMU?
HAZUMU!
PUU!
ぽぽん
POOF
?
SWSH
TOMARIN! HELLO!
GYAAAAA--!
がばっ
SWOP

HA--
GOD! YOU ABSOLUTE PUTZ! DO YOU HAVE ANY IDEA HOW WORRIED I... I MEAN, WE WERE?!
NO... NEVERMIND THAT.
YOU'RE SAFE. THAT'S ALL THAT MATTERS.
HAZUMU ...?
I KNOW, AND I'M SORRY. I SHOULDN'T HAVE JUST SHOWED UP HERE LIKE THIS.
DAMN STRAIGHT! WHY THE HELL DID YOU COME ALL THE WAY OUT HERE BY YOURSELF FOR, ANYWAY?!
TOMARI-CHAN...

I'M SO SORRY I DIDN'T ANSWER ALL THOSE TIMES YOU CALLED ME!
Jun-Puu-Chan found it for me.
I LOST MY CELLPHONE THIS AFTER-NOON...
Just a minute ago, though.
THIS AFTERNOON?
I'VE BEEN CALLING YOU SINCE YESTERDAY.
W-WELL... I... UM...
THAT IS...
I-I WAS WITH YASUNA-CHAN ALL DAY YESTERDAY AND...!
YEAH. I KNOW.
HOW ...?!
AYUKI CALLED ME, SAID SOMETHING CAME UP AND SHE COULDN'T GO. SO IT WAS JUST YOU AND YASUNA ALL DAY, RIGHT?
SO? NO BIGGIE. YOU DON'T HAVE TO GET SO--

WHAT HAPPENED...?
....
UM...
WELL...
—
YOU KNOW...
YASUNA IS LIKE THE *PERFECT* GIRL. LOOK UP "FEMININE" IN THE DICTIONARY, AND YOU'D FIND HER PICTURE.
SHE'S SO PRIM AND PROPER, SO LOVELY AND NICE.
I'M...
NOT LIKE HER.
BUT...
I'M NOT PRETTY, OR PROPER.

I'M NOT GOING TO LOSE TO HER.
PU!
PU!
MMPH MMPH
PUU!
PU?
HRM.

PUUUU...

Jan-puu's
Onee-nii-sama Observation Diary
PUU!
Special #1
Onee-nii-sama
Observation Diary
Onee-nii-sama's breasts are soft and warm and feel really nice!
Jan-puu likes sleeping with Onee-nii-sama.
NN...
NNH...
NUZZLE...

FLOOSH
?!
WHAT THE HECK ARE YOU TWO DOING?!
HEH HEH HEH...
NPH?
SNAP
SNAP
SNAP
HUH...?
WHA...?
HAZUMU, YOU'RE THE BEST!!
HM. THESE ARE SOME VERY INTERESTING SAMPLES...
I HAVE THE BEST GIRL IN THE WORLD!
WOULD YOU TWO...
NUZZLE
ACK!
NO!
JEEZ...
JAN-PUU-CHAN! STOP IT ALREADY. PLEASE?
SNAP SNAP SNAP SNAP
FLOOSH
OOOOOOH!!

KRAAAK
waaaah
ONEE-NII-SAMA...
JAN-PUU THOUGHT "SUMMER VACATION" MEANT THAT ONEE-NII-SAMA WOULD STAY HOME.
WELL, NORMALLY THAT'S TRUE. BUT THERE ARE A FEW DAYS WHERE STUDENTS HAVE TO GO TO SCHOOL.
NOOO!
JAN-PUU WANTS TO PLAY WITH ONEE-NII-SAMA DURING ALL OF VACATION!
SORRY, JAN-PUU-CHAN.
BUT I CAN'T. I HAVE TO GO.
PU...
PUUUU...
HAZUMU, I'LL WALK WITH YOU PART OF THE WAY.
WOW, YOU'RE UP PRETTY EARLY THIS MORNING, DAD.

PUU!
INTERSTELLAR TRAVEL REGULATIONS ACT, ARTICLE 32, PARAGRAPH 4...
WHEN RESIDING WITHIN AN ALIEN STAR-SYSTEM, NEITHER A SPACE SHIP, NOR A SENTIENT PART THEREOF, SHALL TAKE ANY ACTION WITHOUT THE EXPRESS PER-MISSION OF ITS MASTER.
PUUUUUU!
HEY, HAZUMU...?
I KNOW YOUR MOM AND I *KINDA* GOT CARRIED AWAY WITH YOU BEING A GIRL NOW AND ALL...
BUT SERIOUSLY, HOW ARE YOU DOING? ARE YOU OKAY WITH IT?
UMM...
WELL, I CAN'T SAY THERE HAVEN'T BEEN TIMES WHEN I'VE BEEN *TOTALLY* CONFUSED...

BUT I'M OKAY.
I MEAN, IT'S NOT LIKE THERE'S ANY HOPE I'LL GET TURNED BACK, ANYWAY.
AND ALL MY FRIENDS TREAT ME LIKE THEY ALWAYS DID, SO I CAN *DEAL* WITH IT.
HAZUMU!
SEE?
blush

YEAH... I SEE...
IT'S... IT'S *WONDERFUL* HAVING A DAUGHTER.
NO.
YOU STAY OVER HERE.
HUH?
YOU'D WRECK THE PICTURE.
WHA?!!
CUTENESS IS EVERYTHING!!

No arguing that point...
WE'VE GOT SWIMMING CLASS TODAY. DID YOU REMEMBER YOUR SWIMSUIT, HAZUMU?
YEP.
SWIMSUIT?!
THIS'LL BE THE FIRST TIME IN ONE OF THE SCHOOL'S SWIMSUITS
I'm kinda nervous.
true...
EEEE
SCHOOL SWIMSUITS?!!
slump
LATER, DAD.
SEE YOU AFTER WORK.
SWISH
....
WHAT IS IT THAT YOUR FATHER DOES AGAIN...?
HE'S A CAMERA-MAN.
OH.
NOOOOOOO
Now they get it...
なっとく。

sneak sneak
In the end, Jan-puu didn't ask Master for permission to leave.
Because Jan-puu really, really, really wanted to play with Onee-nii-sama today!
PUU!

PUU... ♡
DIING DONG DIING DONG
HELLO, EVERYONE!
HOW HAVE YOU BEEN?
I BET YOU'RE ALL HOT! HERE, LET ME GET YOU SOME WATER!
PUU. ♡

OSARAGI.
OH, HI, CAPTAIN.
YOU'RE EARLY TODAY.
I'VE GOT SWIMMING CLASS TODAY, SO I FIGURED, BETTER TO DO THIS *NOW* RATHER THAN LATER.
YOU WERE TALKING TO THE PLANTS AGAIN, WEREN'T YOU?
HUH? YOU HEARD THAT?
DIDN'T YOU KNOW?
TALKING TO PLANTS AND LETTING THEM LISTEN TO MUSIC AND STUFF LIKE THAT HELPS THEM TO GROW.
OH? NO WONDER ALL THE PLANTS YOU RAISE TURN OUT TO BE SO ***BEAUTIFUL*** AND ***VIBRANT***, HAZUMU-SEMPAI!
YEAH. YOU DIDN'T CHANGE MUCH AT ALL WHEN YOU WERE TURNED INTO A GIRL.
R-REALLY?
DO YOU REALLY THINK SO?

JEEZ.
AND THANKS TO THAT, I'M THE ONLY GUY LEFT IN THE CLUB.
BUT HAZUMU-SEMPAI WAS ALWAYS CUTER THAN OTHER GIRLS, EVEN WHEN SHE WAS A BOY!
C'MON GUYS, KNOCK IT OFF. PLEASE...?
PUU.
Onee-nii-sama has lots and lots of friends besides Tomarin and Yasunan.
They all get along super well.
But Jan-puu thinks...
that Onee-nii-sama all by herself is good enough.

HAZUMU, WHAT'S WRONG?
HUH? OH... NOTHING.
ARE YOU SURE I DON'T LOOK WEIRD?
I GUESS I'M JUST A LITTLE EMBARRASSED ABOUT BEING IN ONE OF THESE GIRLS' SWIM-SUITS...
not at all.

YOU LOOK ADORABLE, HAZUMU-KUN.
I... I DO?
WOO-HOO!!
THANK YOU, SUMMER!!
WHAP WHAP
ALL RIGHT, KIDS! FREE SWIM!
FWEET

ジャ
SPLISH
ジャ
SPLISH
UGH
ばしゃ
SPLOOSH
SPLOOSH
RAAAAAH!
GOD... WHAT'S SO *HARD* ABOUT LEARNING THE CRAWL STROKE...?
WELL?!
YOU'RE STILL JUST *FLAILING*...
URK!
HUFF HUFF

Onee-nii-sama looks like she's having lots of fun.
WHEN WAS THE LAST TIME I ENJOYED SCHOOL SWIMMING CLASSES *THIS* MUCH...?
ELEMENTARY SCHOOL? PROBABLY...
Ha Ha
HAZUMU...
Jan-puu wants to play too.
WE'RE *BEST* FRIENDS, RIGHT? FRIENDS LOOK OUT FOR FRIENDS.
SO I'LL STAY HERE AND BE YOUR LIFEGUARD, JUST IN CASE YOU *MIGHT* START TO DROWN.
Already drowning in Hazumu-Kun.

AND... IF I *DID* HAVE TO RESCUE YOU FROM DROWNING...
THEN I'D HAVE TO PERFORM CPR ON YOU...
NNPH!
WHAT'RE YOU DOING OUT HERE, ASUTA?
AREN'T YOU GOING TO GET IN?
SPLOOT
ARGH!
HUH?!
WH-WHOA!

PUU!
KA-SPLOOOOOSH
HAZUMU!!
HAZUMU!!
HAZUMU-KUN!

ガボガボ
BLURBLE
BLURBLE
BLURBLE
MMPH...
OSARAGI!!
OH MY GOD!
KYAAA
HAZUMU-KUN!
PU...
PU...

PUUUUUUUU!!

PULL!

……
UGK!
KOFF
KOFF
HUH ...?
WHAT THE HECK ...?

WAAAAAAAH!
ONEE-NII-SAMAAA!
JAN-PUU IS SO HAPPY THAT ONEE-NII-SAMA IS OKAY!!
えーん WAAAAH
えーん WAAAAH
えーん WAAAAH
......?
Jan-puu is really happy that Onee-nii-sama was okay.
Onee-nii-sama praised Jan-puu lots and lots.

But...
THAT WAS A BREACH OF THE INTER-STELLAR TRAVEL REGULATION ACT, JAN-PUU.
PUU...
HEY!
WAIT A MINUTE!
SHE DID THAT TO RESCUE ME!
YES. HOWEVER, RULES...
ARE...
RULES.
YOU WILL NEED TO BE PUNISHED.
PUUUUUU!
HUG
Snf
Snf
HRM...

SO WHY IS IT A SWIMSUIT PHOTO SHOOT?!
SNAP
PUU. ♡
SNAP
HAZUMU, YOU'RE THE BEST!!
SNAP
SNAP
AND WHY ME TOO...?
AND WHAT'S ASUTA DOING HERE?!
SNAP
GUYS, ENOUGH ALREADY!!
Today was lots and lots of fun!
No matter what happens, Jan-puu likes Onee-nii-sama the bestest!

かしまし ～ガール・ミーツ・ガール～
KASHIMASHI ~Girl meets Girl~
3かんにつづく
To be continued in volume 3
Observing Japanese high school girls...

JAPANESE HONORIFICS GUIDE

To ensure that all character relationships appear as they were originally intended, all character names have been kept in their original Japanese name order with family name first and given name second. For copyright reasons, creator names appear in standard English name order.

In addition to preserving the original Japanese name order, Seven Seas is committed to ensuring that honorifics—polite speech that indicates a person's status or relationship towards another individual—are retained within this book. Politeness is an integral facet of Japanese culture and we believe that maintaining honorifics in our translations helps bring out the same character nuances as seen in the original work.

The following are some of the more common honorifics you may come across while reading this and other books:

-san – The most common of all honorifics, it is an all-purpose suffix that can be used in any situation where politeness is expected. Generally seen as the equivalent to Mr., Miss, Ms., Mrs., etc.

-sama – This suffix is one level higher than "-san" and is used to confer great respect upon an individual.

-dono – Stemming from the word "tono," meaning "lord," "-dono" signifies an even higher level than "-sama," and confers the utmost respect.

-kun – This suffix is commonly used at the end of boys' names to express either familiarity or endearment. It can also be used when addressing someone younger than oneself or of a lower status.

-chan – Another common honorific. This suffix is mainly used to express endearment towards girls, but can also be used when referring to little boys or even pets. Couples are also known to use the term amongst each other to convey a sense of cuteness and intimacy.

Sempai – This title is used towards one's senior or "superior" in a particular group or organization. "Sempai" is most often used in a school setting, where underclassmen refer to upperclassmen as "sempai," though it is also commonly said by employees when addressing fellow employees who hold seniority in the workplace.

Kouhai – This is the exact opposite of "sempai," and is used to refer to underclassmen in school, junior employees at the workplace, etc.

Sensei – Literally meaning "one who has come before," this title is used for teachers, doctors, or masters of any profession or art.

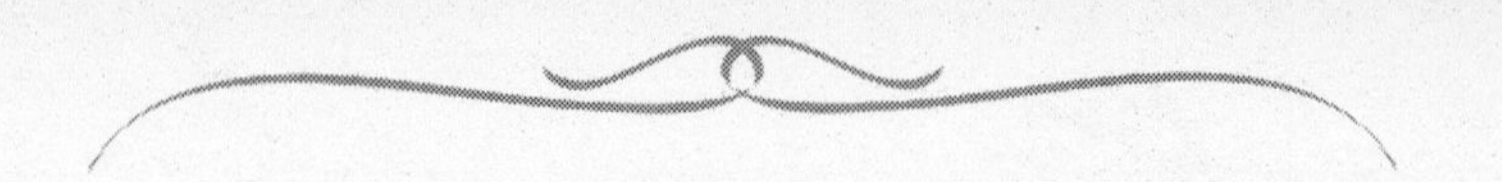

Oniisan – This title literally means "big brother." First and foremost, it is used by younger siblings towards older male siblings. It can be used by itself or attached to a person's name as a suffix (-niisan). It is often used by a younger person toward an older person unrelated by blood, but as a sign of respect. Other forms include the informal "oniichan" and the more respectful "oniisama."

Oneesan – This title is the opposite of "Oniisan" and means "big sister." Other forms include the informal "oneechan" and the more respectful "oneesama."

TRANSLATION NOTES

■ Page 53, Panel 3
"*Obon*" is the Japanese Festival of the Dead and is the second largest family holiday in Japan next to New Year's. Families gather together to honor deceased family members with traditional dances and feasting. Obon is celebrated in mid-July or mid-August, depending on which part of the country you are in.

■ Page 83, Panel 5
Jan-Puu has this tendency to condense honorifics, so she often calls Yasuna and Tomari by the names "*Yasunan*" and "*Tomarin*."

■ Page 103, Panel 2
"*Kami*" means "deity" or "spirit."

■ Page 104, Panel 1
"*Yukata*" is a lightweight type of kimono meant to be worn in summer. They are usually more brightly patterned than kimonos.

■ Page 106, Panel 5
"*Sekihan*" is rice cooked with red beans. Besides being considered very healthy, parents often serve it when they feel their child has made a significant step towards adulthood.

■ Page 113, Panel 4
"*Takoyaki*" are fried dough-balls with bits of octopus inside.

■ Page 161, Panel 5
"*-Obasan*" is sometimes given as an honorary title towards a respected mother figure. This is just what happens when "Tomari calls Hazumu's mom "Osaragi-obasan."

Venus versus Virus
★ヴィーナス ヴァーサス ヴァイアラス★
"Welcome to Venus Vangard.
We've been eXpecting you..."
Open for business June '07

Cat girls, cat girls and more cat girls!
NECONOCLASM
ネコノクラスム
Follow the adventures of more cat-eared cuties than you can shake a stick at in one side-splittingly hilarious volume coming July 2007!

VOLUME 2

story by Satoru Akahori art by Yukimaru Katsura
original character design Sukune Inugami

STAFF CREDITS

translation	**Adrienne Beck**
adaptation	**Janet Houck**
lettering	**Nicky Lim**
retouch	**Cheese**
design & layout	**Nicky Lim**
editor	**Adam Arnold**
publisher	**Seven Seas Entertainment**

Visit us online at www.gomanga.com

ISBN: 978-1-933164-45-8

Printed in Canada

First printing: February 2007

10987654321

THE END

YOU'RE READING THE WRONG WAY

This is the last page of
Kashimashi Volume 2.

This book reads from right to left, Japanese style. To read from the beginning, flip the book over to the other side, start with the top right panel, and take it from there.

If this is your first time reading manga, just follow the diagram. It may seem backwards at first, but you'll get used to it! Have fun!